The Problem of War
in the
Old Testament

Philip Jenson

Lecturer in Old Testament, Ridley Hall, Cambridge

GROVE BOOKS LIMITED
RIDLEY HALL RD CAMBRIDGE CB3 9HU

Contents

First Impression September 2002
Revised Edition July 2010
ISSN 1365–490X
ISBN 978 1 85174 509 8

The 'Problem' of War in the Old Testament

It hardly needs to be demonstrated that wars and rumours of war will be as much a feature of the twenty-first century as every other century before. Recent conflicts in Iraq, Afghanistan, Gaza and elsewhere have caused untold suffering. The so-called war on terrorism has both broadened and complicated the discussion.[1] Applying a Christian perspective has not proved easy, and the church's voice has often been absent or ambiguous. This is hardly surprising since every war is the result of a complex mix of causes, and its conduct is characteristically marked by tragic moral ambiguity, however right the cause. Yet it is of deep concern that there is so little reflection on war from a biblical point of view. An immediate difficulty is that the New Testament has little to say about war. The Old Testament, on the other hand, has a great deal to say about war,[2] but much of it is offensive to the modern reader.

How can this warlike God be the same divinity as the God of love incarnate in Jesus Christ?

The purpose of this booklet is partly apologetic. The Old Testament approach to war is a significant stumbling block both for Christians and non-Christians as they try to get to grips with the Bible. This is particularly the case when we look back over the centuries, and see how Old Testament texts have been used (or rather, misused) to justify very dubious wars, such as the crusades or the 'war' against the native Indian cultures of North America.[3] Further, this is not just an ethical issue but a theological one. How can the warlike God of the Old Testament be the same divinity as that revealed in the New Testament, the God of love incarnate in Jesus Christ?

It is no wonder that there is a growing trend to condemn the Old Testament approach to war. At the end of a recent survey, Cyril Rodd writes,

> In the Old Testament war was not only accepted but religion commonly both justified it and intensified its evil. This view of war is irredeemable.[4]

In a characteristically postmodern move, David Clines reverses the normal point of view readers take to the biblical text and adopts the point of view of the MLF, the Moabite Liberation Front. He writes of Psalm 2.

It is a sad day for theism if the only language its adherents can find to express their sense of the divine is the language of oriental despotism, with its scornful deity who offers comfort to petty kings in their grandiose ambitions and authorizes state violence and a regime of terror against those who want nothing more gross than self-determination.[5]

It is easy, very easy, to dismiss the Old Testament and its God because of the attitude to war. To the modern reader it may seem self-evident. But this should make us pause. Is such an immediate reaction *too easy*? The danger is that we so rapidly stamp our own views onto the text that it becomes hard to read the text in its cultural and biblical context. For example, I am doubtful that 'self-determination' was a significant concept for either the Moabites or the Israelites. Anachronistic responses are invariably superficial from several perspectives.

A Superficial Understanding of Scripture

The problem about treating this biblical text or that as defective or substandard is knowing where to draw the line. Recent attempts to distinguish acceptable and unacceptable texts on ethical grounds are variations of the ancient heresy of Marcionism. The second century theologian Marcion rejected the Old Testament as containing views contradictory to the New Testament, and concluded that it spoke of a different God. However, so many New Testament texts reflected the same ideas that he ended up by rejecting a good proportion of the New Testament as well.[6] Deciding which parts of the Bible acceptable rapidly becomes a subjective, disputed and futile business. It is also simplistic, for it reduces the range of evidence that is necessary in order to do justice to the character of a God who (as I shall argue) cannot be dismissed either as a hawk or a dove.

A Superficial Construal of the Character of God

Doubt about the Old Testament God of war is one aspect of a much bigger question: 'Is the God of the Old Testament the same as the God of the New Testament?' We may not think they are alike, but the starting point for Jesus, his followers, and Christians down the ages, has been the belief that it is the same God who speaks yesterday, today and forever. One difficulty is that we can read both the Old and the New Testaments in a selective way. The Old Testament contains foundational affirmations of the love and justice of God, while some of the most terrible words of hell and condemnation are found on the lips of Jesus. If we are to avoid idolatry (constructing a god we would prefer) we have to deal with the full biblical testimony to the character of God.

A Superficial Approach to the Challenge of Interpretation

The difficulty readers have in making sense of these texts drives us to ask fundamental questions about how we interpret the Bible. What is needed is a framework of interpretation within which specific verses can be understood. It is all too easy to quote Scripture out of context, as Satan did to Jesus in the wilderness. What I hope to do in this booklet is to sketch an approach that will help us interpret the Old Testament texts on war in their own context, in the light of the New Testament, and for today.

Specifically I would like to argue that the OT approach to war is deliber-

An approach that will help interpret the texts in their own context, in the light of the New Testament, and for today

ately *complex, ambivalent, conditional* and *incomplete*. I shall attempt to show this by looking at four key texts about war, drawn from different parts of the Bible and from different kinds of writing (Ex 15; Deut 20; 1 Sam 17; Jer 21). These will introduce broader discussions of the biblical material.

My approach will be canonical and contextual. The *canonical* approach has as its starting and end point the final form of the canonical text. There has been much historical critical discussion of these texts, asking when they were written and how they relate to the history of Israel. For example, there is a lively debate as to whether Israel conquered the land, or infiltrated it peacefully.[7] However, this debate does not help in the task of interpreting the canonical text, which clearly affirms a God who commands all-out war. Yet it is also important to discuss the biblical texts not in isolation,[8] but as part of a much larger canon of Scripture that also includes the New Testament and a common vision of a future rule of peace.

The *contextual* approach to Scripture seeks to do justice to the historical, literary and theological character of the text. But the context of the reader is also a crucial factor. Our interpretations are often unconsciously influenced by larger, underlying assumptions. That this is an important factor is suggested not least by the observation that although war is a problem for us, in both the Old and New Testaments it is simply assumed to be the inescapable order of things.[9] Understanding and examining the underlying assumptions of both text and reader is as important as a careful reading of specific texts.

2

Exodus 15:
The LORD is a Man of War

The first 'war' we shall look at is that between Israel and Egypt. Or rather, it is between Pharaoh and the God of Israel, the LORD (YHWH). Moses may be a great man, but all the initiatives and the decisive military moves come from the LORD. After the tenth and final plague, Pharaoh sends the Israelites away, but then changes his mind and sends his army after them. Moses and the Israelites come to the Red Sea, whose waters are miraculously parted. They cross over safely, but Pharaoh's armies are overthrown by the returning waters.

The Song of the Sea (Exodus 15) is a celebration of this military victory in the extravagant poetry of praise. At its heart is a stark description of God's character: 'The LORD is a warrior; the Lord is his name (v 3).' Most modern translations have 'The LORD is a warrior,' but the usual word for warrior is different (*gibbor*). What we have here (so AV) is literally 'man of war (*'ish milchama*),' the phrase also used to describe Goliath (1 Sam 17.33).

The Exodus is the OT equivalent of the gospel, the central story of God's saving work. The Exodus pattern will be repeated in different keys again and again through the rest of the Bible. So the significance of this passage cannot be exaggerated. This is no minor trait of God that can be passed over.[10] It expresses a foundational assumption of the Old Testament about what YHWH is like. It is natural to use of him verbs such as 'fight' (Ex 14.25; Deut 1.30). He is the commander under whom Israel can attack and defeat the enemy (Deut 9.3). An important title is YHWH *tseva'oth*, LORD of hosts, and these hosts are military forces, whether earthly or heavenly (1 Sam 17.45; Isa 6.3). In this poem key theological terms such as 'glory,' 'strength,' 'salvation' and 'God' are given a military grounding.

Yet at the same time the way in which the LORD wins his victories is most unusual. Note the following points.

There is No Actual Fighting by the Israelites

In Exodus 14.13–14 Moses speaks to the people:

> Do not be afraid, stand firm, and see the deliverance that the LORD will accomplish for you today; for the Egyptians whom you see today you shall never see again. The LORD will fight for you, and you have only to keep still.

The Exodus in this respect is no ordinary war, where men fight one another with weapons and one side wins with the help of superior numbers, motivation, strategy or technology. The means of victory here is entirely supernatural, and from a military point of view the Israelites are entirely passive. This is because the LORD makes use of supernatural weapons (the cosmic floods, the angel of death) and not human armament.

Such an absolute divine victory is found just a few times in the OT, for example, in the miraculous delivery of Hezekiah from the Assyrian army (1 Kings 17). This approach is worked out in a systematic way in Chronicles (for example 2 Chr 20), and has been described as reflecting an ideology of non-participation in war.[11] The presence of this kind of victory in Israel's foundational story gives it a certain priority.[12] God's victory is both spectacular and necessary, given that the Israelites are in such a desperate position of weakness, and highlights that salvation is supremely the result of God's grace and power

The Story Demonstrates the Justice of God

The starting point of the story is an oppressed nation. God listens to the Israelites as they cry out at the injustice of their situation (Ex 3.9) and acts so as to bring about a just resolution of their complaint. But this cannot be by legal means, for no human law court can bring Pharaoh to book. As absolute king he is lord high judge and executioner, without any right to appeal. Yet Pharaoh is not God, and he too is subject to a fundamental principle that is at the heart of the law and indeed of the world order. This is the *lex talionis*, the law of equivalent retribution, an eye for an eye, a tooth for a tooth (Ex 21.24; Lev 24.20; Deut 19.21).

We can see this fundamental principle of justice worked out in the Exodus narrative, particularly in the ironic use of water. The story begins with Pharaoh putting to death Israelite males by drowning them in the water of the Nile (Ex 1.22). The parents of Moses do in fact obey this command to the letter, but with an ingenious twist. They ensure that Moses is thrown into the Nile in a basket, with the result that he is saved by Pharaoh's daughter. The first plague affects the key water source of Egypt, the Nile (Ex 7.14–24). But this only anticipates the most fearful use of water as an instrument of judgment on the hosts of Pharaoh at the Red Sea (Ex 14.21–31). The medium by which Pharaoh brought death to the Israelites is now the means by which his army experiences death. Justice is seen to be done on the largest scale.

> 'An eye for an eye, a tooth for a tooth' is a fundamental principle worked out in the Exodus narrative

There is a Corporate Understanding of Human Nature

We are not told that Pharaoh himself is killed. What justice is there when those not directly responsible for Israel's oppression, Pharaoh's army, are destroyed? Were not at least some innocents caught up in this terrible tragedy? In order to respond to this accusation it is necessary to examine the way in which the assumptions of these ancient texts clash with assumptions that Western culture has come to hold only relatively recently.

The relatively recent assumptions of modern Western culture clash with those of these ancient texts The last three or four centuries of philosophical debate and cultural change have increasingly emphasized an individualistic approach to human nature and society.[13] Today we tend to read the Bible as a book written for individuals by individuals. But most of the Bible, New as well as Old Testaments, takes its starting point in the corporate. In the Exodus story it is Egypt as a corporate whole against Israel as another corporate whole.

A related assumption with which this narrative clashes is the modern stress on the equality of every individual. The traditional political, religious and social assumption is that blessing or curse is channelled through the king or leader of the people. The king acts for the nation, for better—and for worse. A good king maintains justice and is the focus for the ethos and identity of the people. A bad king will lead the country into idolatry, defeat, poverty and destruction. Like king like people. This is the pattern we see worked out in the books of Samuel and Kings, and is reflected in the royal Psalms (for example Ps 72). We see it worked out just as effectively today, when a Hitler, a Churchill, or a Mugabe can embody and set the tone of a nation. The basic truths of representation and solidarity also underlie a Christian understanding of the person and work of Christ. At least they must if the death and resurrection of Christ is to be anything more than the eccentric behaviour of an isolated individual and of no further relevance to anyone.

Pharaoh may be the one primarily responsible for the oppression of Israel, but all suffer along with him. Every firstborn dies. The innocent are caught up along with the guilty because they are linked by bonds of nation and kinship. Individuals can, however, decide to act contrary to the expected norm, as was the case for some of Pharaoh's officials (Exod 9.20–21), for Rahab (Josh 6.17) and for Ruth the Moabite (Ruth 1.16–17). Even this, however, involves the choice for one group rather than another and tends to be the exception and not the rule. The thought and behavioural patterns of both Old and New Testaments are primarily corporate.

The Story Embodies a Symbolic Dimension

It is significant that Pharaoh is not given a specific name. He is not so much an historical individual (*eg* Ramases II) as the embodiment of a royal ideology that seeks to maintain its own power and privilege and refuses to attend to the true God. In his will to power, his reliance on self, he embodies the principle of anti-life.[14] The Exodus story shows in a tragic way and with growing intensity how all that Pharaoh touches leads to death and destruction—of his land, his people, his army, and his own family. The Song of the Sea in Exodus 15 is a song of triumph not so much over a specific nation or individual, but over the forces of chaos and anti-life. This is why cosmic imagery invades the account of the triumph in Exodus 15.4–5:

> Pharaoh's chariots and his army he cast into the sea;
>   his picked officers were sunk in the Red Sea.
> The floods covered them;
>   they went down into the depths like a stone.

This symbolic dimension universalizes the story. Yet the rescue from Egypt is also unique and unrepeatable, for the LORD is acting to create a people for himself that will be distinct from all other peoples (Ex 19.5–6). The Exodus is attended by miracles and plagues that will never be seen again in such number or intensity. As such the story cannot be readily applied to every group that suffers poverty or oppression (as many liberation theologians have done). It is a matter of observation that God does not step in and overthrow tyrants in a supernatural way, or rescue all who cry to him. Although the story does say vital things about the character of God and human beings, this does not determine what should or will happen in other times and places.

3

Deuteronomy 20:
The Rules of War

There are many texts in the Old Testament that describe terrible actions during wars. However, it is not always clear that they are sanctioned by God. Modern readers often assume that the narrator approves of what is being described. However, the biblical narrators often hide their own ethical opinions and expect readers to draw their own conclusions.[15] Nevertheless, there are some texts where God directly commands the Israelites to destroy the nations who occupied the promised land. These bring to mind the terrible genocides that have punctuated the history of the world. There are a number of such texts in Joshua, but of even greater concern is the general instruction found in the laws of conquest and of war. The most important of these are set out in Deuteronomy 20, which describes four different situations.[16]

1 When The Israelites Face Another (and More Powerful) Army: Deuteronomy 20.1–9

The starting point would appear to be a desperate military situation: 'When you go out to war against your enemies, and see horses and chariots, an army larger than your own' (v 1). The key question in most wars is who has the most firepower (Lk 14.31). The ancient equivalent of cruise missiles and cluster bombs were horses and chariots. They were the products of financial and technological superiority and allowed cavalry and charioteers to kill from above or at a distance. It is assumed here that Israel has the inferior firepower.

Indeed the situation is made far worse by permission being given to various categories of people to go home: 'Has anyone become engaged to a woman but not yet married her? He should go back to his house, or he might die in the battle and another marry her' (v 7). Military madness! However, similar exemptions on compassionate grounds are to be found today.[17] Family and community are not subordinate to the war effort, the assertion of an absolute ideology of war, but rather the reverse. The primary explanation for the permission, though, reflects Exodus logic:

> Before you engage in battle, the priest shall come forward and speak to the troops, and shall say to them: 'Hear, O Israel! Today you are drawing near to do battle against your enemies. Do not lose heart, or be afraid,

> or panic, or be in dread of them; for it is the LORD your God who goes
> with you, to fight for you against your enemies, to give you victory.'
> Deut 20.2–4

The basic source of Israel's confidence is its covenantal relationship with YHWH, who has promised to fight for them. The only responsibility of Israel is to trust in him and not to fear the enemy. The success of this strategy has already been seen at the Red Sea (Ex 15.1)

> I will sing to the LORD, for he has triumphed gloriously;
> horse and rider he has thrown into the sea.

2 When Israel Attacks a City Outside the Land of Israel: Deuteronomy 20.10–15

When this situation arises the text sets out two alternative possibilities. The first is that the city surrenders, in which case the consequence is forced labour (v 11). Although this does not appear a very happy option, in the context of the ancient world it is a relatively mild form of takeover. In the chilling story from 1 Samuel 11, the people of Jabesh-Gilead ask to be the subjects of Nahash the Ammonite. He replies (v 2) 'On this condition I will make a treaty with you, namely that I gouge out everyone's right eye, and thus put disgrace upon all Israel.' Contrast the surprising advice that the servants of Ben-hadad, the defeated King of Aram, give him (1 Kgs 20.30): 'Look, we have heard that the kings of the house of Israel are merciful kings; let us put sackcloth around our waists and ropes on our heads, and go out to the king of Israel; perhaps he will spare your life.'

If the city resists, however, the men are to be killed (v 13) and the rest are taken as booty, including women and children (v 14). A modern reader will immediately regard this as a totally unacceptable policy. Yet especially in reading the difficult texts, it is crucial that we read it in its own context and recognize the realities of ensuring the survival of a nation in the ancient world. A more lenient approach would very possibly lead to exactly the same problem in a very short while, and serve as an encouragement to other nations to attack Israel, since the result of losing would be almost inconsequential. It is particularly easy for those who have a long history of independence and peace to adopt idealistic and unrealistic views on war. In terms of later analytical categories, it is possible here to see a combination of deterrent, punishment and retribution. Other laws in Deuteronomy also suggest that the intention is the integration of the women and children with Israel (Deut 21.10–14).

The text also indirectly indicates that peaceful life in the land is the norm and the ideal, and that warfare is an aberrant practice. We are not told why such a confrontation is necessary. Since Deuteronomy sets out clear boundaries for Israel's life that are limited to the land, the implication is that this is a response to an aggressive invasion or incursions into the land. A military response is necessary if Israel is to survive. The recurrent possibility of such a threat to Israel's survival is illustrated by the Midianite raids that begin the story of Gideon (Judges 6).

3 When Israel Attacks Cities Within the Land of Israel: Deuteronomy 20.16–18

Here the moral problems are at their most acute. Within the land everything living must be killed: 'You shall annihilate them—the Hittites and the Amorites, the Canaanites and the Perizzites, the Hivites and the Jebusites—just as the LORD your God has commanded' (v 17). This seems to be a direct and totally unacceptable command by God to commit genocide. Yet even here it is important to understand before we condemn.

For a start, 'annihilate' (NRSV) is not a good translation. Behind this is a special Hebrew term (*hrm*) repeated twice in an intensive construction. Compare some other translations: 'you must destroy them under solemn ban' (REB) or 'you must lay them under the curse of destruction' (NJB). I shall use 'ban' to refer to this term. It is a theological rather than a military term, and so important that it will be discussed more fully in the next section.

4 When Israel Besieges a Town: Deuteronomy 20.19–20

War is a destructive activity and encourages the worst expression of sinful human nature. One of the great challenges of rules of law is how to set clear boundaries and limit the destructive potential of war. This appendix to the chapter seeks to do that in a commendable awareness of the ecology of the land. The besieging Israelite armies are only to cut down such trees that they need for the actual siege. A rhetorical question implies that this is not an awareness that comes naturally: 'Are trees in the field human beings that they should come under siege from you?' (v 19).

War is not such an overwhelming priority that it permits the use of any means to achieve an end. It regards humanity (both Israelites and others) as part of a larger, mutually dependent whole. The ignoring of this principle has led to the desertification of a large part of Israel and the Middle East. The recognition of the folly of 'total war' without limitation is a long-term point of view that sets boundaries to present behaviour, however militarily desirable.

The Ban

The ban appears several times in Deuteronomy, but it is important to recognize that law is not necessarily a good guide to practice. Indeed, although scholars have tried to set out a standard pattern for how war was to be waged, the variation in practice is striking. Deuteronomy may well be setting out an ideal rather than a reality. Many historical-critical scholars regard the final form of Deuteronomy as a formulation of the exilic period. Looking back, the failure of Israel to observe its laws was very evident, leading as it did to complete defeat and exile. Hence there was value in explaining this by putting **Deuteronomy may well be setting out an ideal rather than a reality** matters in a clear and extreme way. A canonical view also acknowledges a gap between law and historical reality, but more in the sense that Moses sets forth ideals that need to be realized in the future. The story of Israel indicates that the neglect of these laws was much more common that their execution. Indeed, there appear to be only three clear cases of the ban, and these differ in character amongst themselves (Josh 6–7; 11; 1 Sam 15).

Although these comments put the issue in perspective, the ban remains as a divine command according to the canonical texts. Yet there are several contextual factors that may begin to explain why such an extreme measure was thought to be necessary.

The Ban is a Realistic Solution to the Problem of Idolatry

The reason for the ban in Deuteronomy 20.18 is 'so that they may not teach you to do all the abhorrent things that they do for their gods, and you thus sin against the LORD your God.' The extreme nature of this instruction is therefore a corollary of the deadly seriousness of avoiding idolatry, the first commandment (Deut 5.7–10). The consequence of turning to idolatry is also made clear—the complete destruction of a people (Deut 7.4).

The ban appears to contradict the character of God revealed in the rest of the Bible as loving, just, and merciful to all (Gen 1–11; Jonah). Yet the key contextual issue is whether this extreme measure was the only realistic possibility of creating a society and culture that held fast to the true God. From a larger canonical perspective, what we have here is the tragic necessity to choose the lesser of two evils. The need for such stark laws is a witness to the tendency for human beings to prefer idols to the living God.

What we have here is the tragic necessity to choose the lesser of two evils

Once again, to make such a statement is to begin a serious questioning of modern values. Someone who sets little value on the faith of Israel will not judge such a policy to be defensible. But if the larger purpose is the salvation of the world, then perhaps there was no other alternative. Although we (and God) would much prefer a gentler and less extreme policy, is this an option in the real, fallen world? Unless there is a complete break with the culture of the time, then Israel's covenant faith is threatened with extinction. If there are villages with girls and boys in close proximity, then it is hard to see how it would be possible to prohibit intermarrying and all that this entails in adopting the predominant cultural values. Religion and society were not separate spheres in the ancient world. The deuteronomic laws assume (and the evidence suggests that it was a correct assumption) that the destruction of the people is the only way to destroy their religion, the sacred poles and idols and all they stood for. Only in this way, it is assumed, can the distinctive faith of Israel survive.

This extremism may perhaps shed light on the state of the church in the West today. The devastating power of a society and an ideology that rejects the living God may be quickly and tragically grasped by looking at the lack of teenagers in most congregations. Simply from a statistical point of view, the Church of England (along with most other churches) is losing the battle against Western contemporary culture. But we would not expect anything else if we took Deuteronomy's view seriously. There is a war out there for the hearts and minds of our children, and the tragedy is that the church hardly seems aware of the reasons why it is facing defeat—compromise, a love of tolerance, a lack of confidence in the gospel. There is no book more dedicated to the challenge of educating the next generation in the fear of the Lord than Deuteronomy, and its approach is as radical as the situation is desperate. The faithful are to love the Lord our God with all of our heart and soul and strength, but the other side is the annihilation of anything that will compromise that activity. The most potent weapon in the church's arsenal is the exposure of our young people to a dedicated community that rejects all compromise with the world, and that displays the devotion and rejection of idolatry that is Deuteronomy's ideal for the people of God. The most effective evangelism today takes place when young people can see Christians living in an uncompromising way— Christian camps for young people, or Christian communities such as those in Taizé or Lourdes.

The Ban Excludes Personal Gain

The ban in its purest form requires complete destruction of not only people but also objects. Israel gains nothing from such an activity. This again strikes an unusual note. Although we like to think of war as being waged on high moral grounds, the reality tends to be rather different. Indeed, it could be argued that the main reason for wars of aggression is plunder and the power that wealth brings. Note the glee with which Sennacherib describes the results of his 701 BC campaign

> Hezekiah himself...did send me, later, to Nineveh, my lordly city, together with 30 talents of gold, 800 talents of silver, precious stones, antimony, large cuts of red stone, couches (inlaid) with ivory, *nimedu*-chairs (inlaid) with ivory, elephant-hides, ebony-wood, boxwood (and) all kinds of valuable treasures, his (own) daughters and concubines, male and female musicians.[18]

There are many who would point to Western capitalism and its correlative materialism as the primary form idolatry takes today.

The Ban and 'Holy' War

The ban is an overtly religious concept, often related to the idea of purity.[19] In the literature it is frequently related to the concept of the 'holy war.'[20] Yet this phrase is never found in the Bible, and Jones has argued persuasively that we should really speak of a 'Yahweh war.'[21] Yes, God is Lord of war. But he is also the living God, there is a significant distance between him and the death that accompanies war. The holiness system of Leviticus does its best to ensure that there is a crucial conceptual and practical distance between God and death in any form.[22] The classic expression of this in relation to war is that David is forbidden to build the temple. Instead his son Solomon, whose name means 'peace,' is chosen (1 Chr 7.27–29; *cf* 1 Kgs 5.3–4):

> David said to Solomon, 'My son, I had planned to build a house to the name of the LORD my God. But the word of the LORD came to me, saying, "You have shed much blood and have waged great wars; you shall not build a house to my name, because you have shed so much blood in my sight on the earth. See, a son shall be born to you; he shall be a man of peace. I will give him peace from all his enemies on every side; for his name shall be Solomon, and I will give peace and quiet to Israel in his days."'

War may be unavoidable, but it was not intended by God from the beginning. It is an aspect of a fallen world that God purposes to redeem. Genesis 1–11 tells the story of spreading sin and the introduction of murder (Gen 4) and violence (Gen 6.11) into God's good world. The coming of the flood marks God's judgment on such behaviour, but the continuing story emphasizes that this was no permanent solution because of humanity's inclination towards sin. It is against this background that the call of Abraham promises something new in the promise of a nation that will make God known (Gen 12.2). From a canonical point of view God's desire to save the world through the descendants of Abraham makes the wars required to establish that nation a necessary evil.

The provisionality of war is at the heart of the prophetic vision of *shalom*, peace (for example Isa 2.4), even though this has to be established through war. The ban is a temporary measure necessary for Israel to be established in the land. War is a temporary measure until God comes to establish justice and peace (see Rev 20.7–10).

The Ban has a Moral Dimension

In Deuteronomy 9.6 the dispossession of the nations is traced to their wickedness. In Genesis 15.16 the LORD tells Abraham that his descendants will only possess the land in the distant future 'for the iniquity of the Amorites is not yet complete.' In Leviticus 18.27 Israel is told to avoid serious sexual sins and offering their offspring to Moloch 'for the inhabitants of the land, who were before you, committed all of these abominations, and the land became defiled.' These texts suggest that the destruction of the nations was seen as a righteous judgment on their corrupt level of life.[23] Just as the Assyrians will be God's means of judgment on sinful Israel, so Israel is the medium for God's punishment of these nations. Again, we have to understand the scope of this matter in the light of the principle of corporate responsibility. God's demand for justice and righteousness is worked out in the political life and death of nations.

We may be uncomfortable with this widespread Old Testament perspective for several reasons. The law is the normal means for the establishment of justice and the punishment of the wicked, and in modern law individuals are tried, not families or nations. Yet it is a matter of observation that the punishment or vindication of an individual will profoundly affect his or her family. The purpose of Israelite law was primarily to maintain and strengthen the underlying social structure of society based on family and faithfulness to God. But what happens when the law itself is undermined? The way in which people are treated in a law court sends powerful messages to the society as a whole about what is regarded as acceptable or unacceptable behaviour. In extreme situations (the Germany of the third Reich, or Zimbabwe under Mugabe) the breakdown of law often signifies the breakdown of society as a whole and the values that are necessary for its maintenance. These basic human values are ultimately based on God's character and will, and the ultimate sanction can only be his judgment. This is worked out in the common human experience of cause and effect, which is evident both on a small scale and on the larger stage of politics and war.

Despite these general truths, we should note that this theme is not a central one in the reasons given for the destruction of the nations. Nor is it evident from the archaeological and literary evidence we have that the various Canaanite nations were so much more wicked than others who lived outside the land. There is a danger that we assume without supporting evidence a particular degree of wickedness in a culture because this was a rhetorical emphasis of the biblical writers in a few texts.[24] Deuteronomy is also very clear that the Israelites cannot claim any moral superiority over the nations (Deut 9). What is decisive is the free election of Israel by the God of all the world and his desire to make his name known. At the same time, we should be aware that blanket approval of a nation's moral state is as superficial as a demonization. There is a relation between religion and morality, and although the primary stress of Deuteronomy is the concern to ensure the worship of the LORD alone, this has crucial implications for ethical behaviour (as is evident in the structure and unity of the Ten Commandments). The moral dimension is thus significant, but only one aspect of the ban.

The Ban is an 'Incomprehensible Counsel'

The various perspectives we have considered go some way (perhaps a long way) to explaining the necessity of the ban. However, a convincing rationale for the necessity of the associated innocent suffering may be as hidden to us as it was to Job. It is probably right to acknowledge that no response is fully persuasive or adequate. The Bible makes a number of general assertions about God that it is difficult for us to reconcile with specific stories. There is an overarching affirmation of his justice and mercy (Gen 18.25; Ex 34.6), but readers down the ages have found it difficult or impossible to reconcile these qualities with certain laws and stories. Yet it is the starting point of a Christian reading of the Bible that we cannot pick and choose. Further, the canonical stress is first of all on the goodness and mercy of God, and it is here we must start and end.

There is indeed an alternative to abandoning the divine inspiration of texts we find hard. Calvin characteristically combines honesty with a deep respect for the God-given Scriptures:[25]

> It seems harsh, nay, barbarous and inhuman, that young children, without fault, should be hurried off to cruel execution, to be stoned and burned…it seems a cruel vengeance to stone and burn children for the crime of their father; and here God publicly inflicts punishment on children for the sake of their parents, contrary to what he declares by Ezekiel…What here remains for us, but to acknowledge our weakness and submit to his incomprehensible counsel?

Calvin is referring to the judgment on an Israelite, Achan (Joshua 7), but it is an attitude that applies more generally to difficult texts. God is a complex character at work in a world we hardly understand, and it is not surprising we cannot grasp fully his actions and purposes.

The argument of this chapter is that the ban is perhaps not as incomprehensible as Calvin implies. Yet it is perhaps just as worrying if Christians do not feel the tragedy and the suffering that is an inevitable consequence of these harsh laws. It forces us to ask about the ends that could possibly justify such practices. From the larger Christian perspective this then becomes a question about the necessity of the coming of Jesus Christ in the fullness of time as a Jew, a member of the nation made possible by these wars. If the Jewish character and context of Jesus Christ is not regarded as of much significance or value, then it is very understandable that the means by which Israel was established are evaluated negatively. This point is all the more significant because modern approaches to Christology frequently bracket or sideline his Jewishness, even though this is the central emphasis of the New Testament.[26]

1 Samuel 17: David and Goliath

Our third text is a masterpiece of Hebrew narrative, the famous story of David and Goliath. The text is a crucial piece in the complex jigsaw of the story of David's rise in the second part of 1 Samuel. The key moment that has captured the imaginations of readers and interpreters is, of course, the defeat of Goliath and the cutting off of his head. But when we look carefully at this key moment in context, we find yet again some intriguing features that tell us more about the complex biblical attitude to war.

Motivation is More Important Than the Battle

The story of David and Goliath begins in 1 Samuel 17.1, but there is an astonishing delay before we come to the battle, which is all over in one verse, verse 48. It is a striking and recurrent feature of the biblical accounts of war that the account leading up to the battle is extensive, while the battle is described with breathtaking brevity.[27] Hollywood would not want to hire our author as a scriptwriter! What matters above all are the motivations of those taking part, and their relation to God. David's story is a positive paradigm of faith and zeal. Saul's fearfulness in this chapter is based on a lack of trust, as is shown by his future behaviour. Ultimately he will consult the spirit of Samuel in a forbidden rite (1 Sam 28), and is he almost paralysed by fear as he approaches his last battle, defeat and death (1 Sam 31). The trust in God demanded of the people in Deuteronomy is now required of the king (see Ps 18; 144).

The Conflict is Theological First and Military Second

The conflict between David and Goliath is not just a battle between two superwarriors. It is almost the reverse in David's case. In accord with best Israelite practice, David enters the battle from a position of weakness: 'You come to me with sword and spear and javelin; but I come to you in the name of the LORD of hosts, the God of the armies of Israel, whom you have defied' (v 45). What matters is not superior military equipment but that Goliath has mocked the living God. He 'cursed David by his gods' (v 43). David counters by an appeal to the living God, who would be little use in these circumstances unless he were indeed 'the LORD of hosts, the God of the armies of Israel' (v 45). What makes all the difference is that the LORD is with David. His lack of stature might appear a weakness, but it is the LORD that shows his true fitness for kingship (1 Sam 16.12–13) in place of the superficially impressive but fearful Saul (1 Sam 10.22–23).

Nor is the *lex talionis* lacking. Goliath promises 'Come to me, and I will give your flesh to the birds of the air and to the wild animals of the field' (v 44). David reverses the threat but acknowledges that the LORD will be the decisive actor: 'This very day the LORD will deliver you into my hand, and I will strike you down and cut off your head; and I will give the dead bodies of the Philistine army this very day to the birds of the air and to the wild animals of the earth' (v 46).

David's primary motivation is one that goes right back to the Exodus. The calling of Israel is to be witness to the cosmic supremacy of the God of Israel: 'so that all the earth may know that there is a God in Israel' (v 46). Through wonderful deeds both Israel (Ex 6.7) and the Egyptians (representing the whole earth) were to know the LORD is the true and living God. In the context of the ancient world, it is difficult to imagine how a pacifist God could have made any sort of impression, either upon Israel or its enemies.

The Battle Takes Place on a Small Scale

The story of 1 Samuel 17 is a story of a battle by chosen representatives of the people, either a champion or a king. David triumphs over the Philistine through strategy, accuracy and courage. Even though a sling is a distance weapon, David would still have had to cast it at close range. In studying the wars of the Bible, it is important to recognize how different warfare is today. This will affect the way we evaluate the character and consequences of war.

It is important to recognize how different warfare is today

A typical fight then would be between tens or hundreds of men, only very rarely thousands. No-one quite knows what to do with the large numbers of the OT, but they are not to be taken as real numbers. An impressive victory by Jonathan is described thus: 'In that first attack Jonathan and his armour-bearer killed some twenty men in an area of about half an acre' (1 Sam 14.14). The invasion of Kuwait ('Operation Desert Storm'), by way of contrast, involved hundreds of thousands of men—and women.

Women take no part in battles in the Bible, unless it is by subterfuge (Judges 4.17–22; Judith 11–13). Hand-to-hand combat required the brute physical strength to wield armour, swords and spears. This is far less the case now that guns and missiles are the order of the day. Other crucial battle qualities were the ability not to panic when face to face with the enemy. A strong motivation was needed to risk an extended and potentially fatal confrontation, with no doctors and nurses around to patch people up.

This kind of war has just about disappeared. The technology has moved on. The dedication of the Taliban counted for little against the American hi-tech arsenal. The ultimate *blitzkrieg* in the ancient world came in the form of horses and chariots, but battle was still basically face-to-face. The enlarged scale of war and increased personal distance has made the ethics of war far more ambiguous and difficult. Only at the cinema can we wholeheartedly cheer James Bond as he overcomes hand-to-hand a supervillain about to destroy the world.

Jeremiah 21

My fourth and final text is one forged in the midst of war, but this time the result will be very different. The texts we have been considering so far have expected Israel to win. Jeremiah, however, has the unenviable task of announcing Israel's divinely decreed defeat to the Babylonians, the superpower of his day.

We begin with the King, Zedekiah, sending Jeremiah a request: 'Please inquire of the LORD on our behalf, for King Nebuchadnezzar of Babylon is making war against us; perhaps the LORD will perform a wonderful deed for us, as he has often done, and will make him withdraw from us' (v 2). The words recall the grand deeds of the past—the Exodus, the conquest, the saving of Jerusalem from the Assyrians. But that 'perhaps' should make us pause. In context it is clear that this is a last ditch strategy when all else has failed. It arises from desperation rather than trust, and contradicts the policies of the king to date.

And yes, God does indeed respond, but in an ominous, inverted key:

> Thus says the LORD, the God of Israel: I am going to turn back the weapons of war that are in your hands and with which you are fighting against the king of Babylon…I myself will fight against you with outstretched hand and mighty arm, in anger, in fury, and in great wrath. And I will strike down the inhabitants of this city, both human beings and animals; they shall die of a great pestilence. Afterward, says the LORD, I will give King Zedekiah of Judah, and his servants, and the people in this city…into the hands of King Nebuchadnezzar of Babylon…He shall strike them down with the edge of the sword; he shall not pity them, or spare them, or have compassion.
>
> (Jeremiah 21.4–7)

Here are the familiar promises of the Yahweh war, but now turned against the king of Jerusalem, David's lesser heir. There remains, however, a choice for individuals. The principle of solidarity means that the city is doomed along with its king, but the prophet states that life in exile is a possible alternative to death in the city:

> And to this people you shall say: Thus says the LORD: See, I am setting before you the way of life and the way of death. Those who stay in this

> city shall die by the sword, by famine, and by pestilence; but those who
> go out and surrender to the Chaldeans who are besieging you shall live
> and shall have their lives as a prize of war. (verses 8–9)

Why does Jeremiah proclaim this great reversal? The following oracle repeats an all too familiar theme:

> To the house of the king of Judah say: Hear the word of the LORD,
> O house of David! Thus says the LORD:
> Execute justice in the morning,
>   and deliver from the hand of the oppressor
>   anyone who has been robbed,
> or else my wrath will go forth like fire,
>   and burn, with no one to quench it,
>   because of your evil doings. (verses 11–12)

Note an authentic and typical prophetic contradiction. The chapter starts off by saying that Zedekiah can hope for nothing. Here there is hope, but it is based not on a military promise but a moral imperative. The call is specifically to the 'house of David,' for the king and heir of David has a special responsibility for sharing the same zeal for justice as David himself. This moral critique is applied not only to Israel but also to other nations in the 'oracles against the nations' (for example Jer 46–51; Amos 1–2). It is assumed that all people have a certain knowledge of how to behave, and violations of this lead to God's wrath and punishment. Such passages are a clear prophetic criticism of nations (including Israel) that do not recognize basic principles of law and justice.

Jeremiah 21 thus contributes several further truths to the Old Testament understanding of war.

- Injustice and immorality compromise the Lord's assurance of his saving presence in war.
- God is free to fight against his people if they reject him. He can use other nations to execute his judgment.
- When the nation is compromised by lack of trust and prevailing injustice, the acceptance of defeat may be the right path.
- The leaders of the people are primarily responsible for war and its consequences (the principle of representation).

The neglect of passages such as this has often compromised wars taken on for mainly political or economic reasons.

A Biblical Theology of War

I hope it has become clearer what I meant in proposing that the Old Testament approach to war is *complex, ambivalent, conditional* and *incomplete*.

Complex

We have seen that God takes a range of stances in relation to Israel's wars:

- God sometimes fights for Israel and then Israel needs only to trust.
- Israel sometimes fights with God's assurance of success.
- Israel's success at war is sometimes tied to the godliness and competence of its king.
- God sometimes uses other nations to wage war against Israel.

Ambivalent

In the OT some wars are by the command of God. Nevertheless there are contradictions and paradoxes that undermine any view of war that regards it as the primary will of God.

- Fighting is necessary, but a fighting king is not allowed to build the temple.
- The LORD is a man of war, but his essential holiness is incompatible with the death associated with war.
- The God of Israel is first of all a God of justice, mercy and compassion, who desires life and peace, not war and death.

Conditional

God's granting of success in war depends on a number of factors, including:

- Trust in the LORD, especially from a position of weakness.
- A society and leadership marked by justice.

Incomplete

This is not something I have emphasized up to this point, because I have first of all wanted to approach the Old Testament on its own terms. But for Christians it comprises only the first part of the biblical canon. It cannot be interpreted apart from the New Testament.

Interpreting the Two Testaments

Very roughly interpreters follow three different approaches to the challenge of how to relate the Old and New Testaments to one another.

1 Emphasizing the Continuity

The Old and the New Testaments have been traditionally understood to refer to the same God, and to communicate the same message. In a Christian nation prime ministers can be assured of church support for a national war, and army chaplains can pray to God for victory. There is a line of continuity from the people of God in the Old Testament to the people of God today, with their armies:

OT ⎯⎯⎯⎯⎯➤ NT ⎯⎯⎯⎯⎯➤

It need hardly be observed that this approach is rarely found today. This is partly because the assumption of Christendom, and the associated close alignment of church and state, no longer holds. We are also more aware of our historical distance from the Old Testament.

2 Emphasizing the Discontinuity

Much more common nowadays is the opposite emphasis on discontinuity. The newness of the New Testament means that the Old Testament is easily regarded as antiquated, primitive (often in a derogatory sense), and irrelevant. Pacifists tend to emphasize the radical changes that have taken place with the coming of Christ.[28] There is such a chasm between the Testaments that the Old Testament approach to war becomes entirely irrelevant.

OT ⎯⎯⎯⎯➤ | |NT ⎯⎯⎯⎯➤

3 Continuity and Discontinuity

I propose that neither of these models is adequate. The New Testament does bring about something new, but in a way that usually demonstrates both continuity and discontinuity. It tends to transform rather than simply carry over or abrogate. Moreover, the new order brought about by Christ is only inaugurated, and much of the old order abides until Christ comes again.

OT ⎯⎯⎯⎯⎯➤ ⎯ ⎯ ⎯ ⎯ ⎯ ⎯➤
　　　　　　　　 NT ⎯ ⎯ ⎯ ⎯ ⎯➤

For example the new order brought about by Christ will eventually mean the end of marriage. But in this present age some Christians are called to marriage and others to celibacy, a distinctive feature of the new order. The same complex overlap of the ages is evident in the church's approach to war. War is to be avoided if at all possible, for Christ comes as prince of peace, but it may be a necessity in the fallen world in which we continue to live. Most would acknowledge that it was right for Britain to enter into the second world war. Yet when Christians are called to take part in war, there are various ways in which the approach to war is transformed. It may well be the case that the New Testament is all the more significant when the conflict involves Christians, or nations with a Christian cultural heritage. But the extensive material in the Old Testament about war in general may be more applicable to contexts where there is little consciousness of the significance of Christ.

Evaluating War

The coming of Christ has transformed key elements of the identity of the people of God. They are no longer defined by race or by land, but by faith in Jesus Christ. Despite Romans 11, I find no justification for any kind of physical Zionism.[29] The radical change in dispensation following Easter means that there is no warrant for applying the nationalistic aspects of the Old Testament, including the Yahweh war, to the church. Christian interpreters have in fact acknowledged this by spiritualizing the wars of the OT. The enemies of today are not nations, or even individuals, but spiritual forces of wickedness in the heavenly places (Eph 6.12). This spiritualization is already evident in the Old Testament, as was noted in the discussion of the symbolic character of Pharaoh. The 'enemies' of the Psalms invite interpretation in an indefinite and metaphorical way. Yet the Old Testament background of real war remains crucial in defining the language of spiritual warfare, and the way in which God interacts with Israel in its wars provides vital indications for how our spiritual battles can become part of God's purposes (or not). For example, we cannot depend on God's help in our fight against sin if we reject his moral demands.

Yet spiritualization is not the only interpretive possibility. At least some of the Old Testament insights into the nature of war offer critical perspectives for evaluating the contemporary ideology and practice of war. Synthesizing points made in relation to the particular passages, areas of concern in assessing whether a war is a greater or lesser evil (if not a 'just' war) might be:

- *The motives for waging war. Some* rulers are so hard-hearted that they serve the forces of anti-life and are subject to God's judgment on themselves and their nation, possibly through war (Ex 20). War should not be waged primarily for economic reasons (Deut 20).

Wars for survival or for the re-establishment of justice are more justifiable.

- *The assumptions about human nature.* These have to include a realistic understanding of power and human nature (1 Sam 17). *Sometimes* military force is the only language that will be understood. *Sometimes* military intervention is justified.

- *The moral framework guiding the conduct of war* (Jer 21). Adherence to rules of war (for example the Geneva convention) and the moral integrity of the leadership of the war are important factors.

- *The wider environmental implications of war.* War should be waged with a due respect for natural resources (Deut 20). It is very difficult to justify certain technologies of war (for example napalm, nuclear bombs) that cause pervasive damage of the environment, as well as indiscriminately injuring the innocent.

A biblical ethic of war will seek to apply and relate the multiple perspectives on war that are evident in both Old and New Testaments. Furthermore it will seek to analyse as fully as possible the complex character of any particular war. The difficulties of the task should not be underestimated. But this prophetic task is required of those who confess the God of the Bible as one who is sovereign over the nations and the righteous judge of all that takes place, both in war and in peace.

Notes

1   For a discussion of whether September 11th is 'war' see R Williams, *Writing in the Dust: Reflections on 11th September and its Aftermath* (London: Hodder & Stoughton, 2002). For a sophisticated poetic and biblical response see Godfrey Rust in *Third Way*, Vol 24/8 November 2001, pp 14-15. For this and other responses see http://chaplains.sa.utoronto.ca/crc/Sept11/ and http://www.sojo.net/special/index.cfm/action/home.html

2   A lively description of the technology of war is given by Y Yadin, *The Art of Warfare in Biblical Lands in the Light of Archaeological Study* (New York/London: McGraw-Hill/Weidenfeld & Nicolson, 1963).

3   See the opening survey in P C Craigie, *The Problem of War in the Old Testament* (Grand Rapids: Eerdmans, 1978); also R H Bainton, *Christian Attitudes Toward War and Peace: A Historical Survey and Critical Re-Evaluation* (London: Hodder and Stoughton, 1961).

4   C S Rodd, *Glimpses of a Strange Land: Studies in Old Testament Ethics* (Edinburgh: T & T Clark, 2000) pp 205-6.

5   D J A Clines, 'Psalm 2 and the MLF (Moabite Liberation Front)' in *Interested Parties: The Ideology of Writers and Readers of the Hebrew Bible* (Sheffield: Sheffield Academic Press, 1995) pp 244-75, 274. Ironically Moab is responsible for the execution of the ban (see chapter 3) on Israelites according to the Moabite stone (ANET p 320; also at http://www2.ida.net/graphics/shirtail/moabite.htm).

6   In relation to war the expulsion of the nations is regarded positively in Acts 7.45; 13.19.

7   See the survey in G W Ramsey, *The Quest for the Historical Israel: Reconstructing Israel's Early History* (London: SCM, 1982).

8   Treating texts in isolation from their context is often characteristic of Clines' approach.

9   T R Hobbs, *A Time for War: A Study of Warfare in the Old Testament* (Old Testament studies 3; Wilmington: Michael Glazier, 1989) p 17.

10 It would not be wise to build too much theology on an individual metaphor (such as 'I am like maggots to Ephraim,' Hos 5.12) but the imagery of Ex 15 is of a different order of importance.

11 S Niditch, *War in the Hebrew Bible: A Study in the Ethics of Violence* (New York/Oxford: Oxford University Press, 1993) pp 134–49.

12 M C Lind, *Yahweh is a Warrior: The Theology of Warfare in Ancient Israel* (Kitchener: Herald Press, 1980) makes this motif primary in his pacifist interpretation of the texts.

13 The literature is vast. See for example the writings of Peter Berger, Colin Gunton, and Tom Wright.

14 T E Fretheim, *Exodus* (Interpretation; Louisville: John Knox, 1991).

15 They are covert rather than overt narrators (S Bar-Efrat, *Narrative Art in the Bible* (Sheffield: JSOT Press, 1989) chapter 1).

16 See the good discussion of the relevant texts in P D Miller, *Deuteronomy* (Interpretation; Louisville: John Knox, 1990); C J H Wright, *Deuteronomy* (NIBC; Peabody, MA: Hendrickson, 1996).

17 See for example the plot of the film *Saving Private Ryan*.

18 See J B Pritchard (ed), *Ancient Near Eastern Texts Relating to the Old Testament* (3rd ed; Princeton, NJ: Princeton University Press, 1969) p 288. In German war (*Krieg*) is related to the verb 'get' (*kriegen*).

19 See S Niditch, *War in the Hebrew Bible: A Study in the Ethics of Violence* (New York/Oxford: Oxford University Press, 1993).

20 See above all G von Rad, *Holy War in Ancient Israel* (Grand Rapids: Eerdmans, 1991 (1958)).

21 G H Jones, "'Holy war' or 'Yahweh war'?" *Vetus Testamentum* 25 (1978) pp 642–58; 'The Concept of Holy War,' in R E Clements (ed), *The World of Ancient Israel* (Cambridge: CUP, 1989) pp 299–321.

22 See P P Jenson, *Graded Holiness: A Key to the Priestly Conception of the World* (Sheffield: JSOT Press, 1992) chapters 2 and 3.

23 J Wenham, *The Goodness of God* (London: Tyndale Press, 1974) pp 119–47. This was reprinted as *The Enigma of Evil: Can We Believe in the Goodness of God?* (2nd ed; Leicester: Inter-Varsity Press, 1985).

24 See D R Hillers, 'Analyzing the Abominable: Our Understanding of Canaanite Religion,' *Jewish Quarterly Review* 75 (1985) pp 253–69.

25 J Calvin, *Commentary on Joshua 7.24*.

26 J Moltmann, *The Way of Jesus Christ: Christology in Messianic Dimensions* (London: SCM, 1990).

27 In Judges 4, Deborah and Barak finally defeat Sisera and his 900 chariots in v 15. But we are not told how, and can only deduce this from allusions in the poem of the following chapter. Similarly in Judges 11, the extended diplomacy between Jephthah and the Ammonites is described, until a bare 'the LORD gave them into his hand' (v 32). See also the lack of any fighting in the final triumph of Revelation 19.20.

28 O R Barclay in his contribution to the essays he edited, *Pacifism and War: Eight Prominent Christians Debate Today's Issues* (Leicester: Inter-Varsity Press, 1984), highlights the importance of hermeneutics (p 215).

29 See C Chapman, *Whose Promised Land? The continuing crisis over Israel and Palestine* (Oxford: Lion 2002) for a wide-ranging discussion of Christian attitudes to the land of Israel.